VOL. 1

LEARN TO DRAW

ART DECO STYLE

KAREN CAMPBELL

Return to the roaring 20's and 30's and learn how to draw and color
female fashion figures, faces, hair, accessories, shoes and more!

A FEW WORDS...

The best little nugget of wisdom I ever heard was, "make the books you'd want for yourself". THIS is exactly what you are holding in your hot little hands. This is my 10th book to date and the first one that I'm publishing purely for selfish reasons. Those 4 reasons being: I LOVE history (and all things vintage!). I LOVE art. I LOVE fashion illustration. I LOVE teaching. This book is the perfect amalgamation of all four. I truly hope you enjoy digesting the content as much as I did cultivating its deliciousness.

Nothing is worse than a drawing book where the images are so small you can't see each step! Or where too many steps are skipped. In this book, you'll find clear, step-by-step instructions, large images and helpful links so that you can truly follow along!

You may be interested to know that all of the full figures you see in this book were adapted from actual fashion sketches as they appeared in magazines, sales catalogues or sewing patterns during the Art Deco Period (roughly 1920-1940). All of these images are in the Public Domain either because they were published prior to 1924 or because the images were never formally registered with the United States Copyright Office at the point of publication.

I had to do a lot of research for this book and credit the following websites for providing additional factual information and or inspiration: smithsonianmag.com, vintagedancer.com, fascinationstreetvintage.wordpress.com, wikipedia, violetsvintagevault.wordpress.com, thevintagetraveler.wordpress.com and glamourdaze.com.

For a list of my favorite art supplies: www.amazon.com/shop/karencampbellartist

WOMEN'S FASHION

The end of the first world war marked the era of "the new woman".

Fashion in the 1920's became much more loose and comfortable than it had ever been!

Women adopted a freer spirit as well! It was a time of change.

Coco Chanel got rid of the restrictive corset and introduced real and faux pearls!

Waistlines dropped to allow a lot more freedom of movement while hemlines rose to accommodate the high kicking Charleston!

Ladies cut their hair. They also worked, drove, smoked, and finally exercised their right to vote.

Let's have fun while learning to draw some of these fun fashion figures of the 20's and 30's!

THE DAY DRESS

1920's **Day Dresses** were worn while women were out running errands, visiting friends or going to work.

Most day dresses were long sleeved or bell sleeved, whereas evening dresses were almost always sleeveless.

Drawing 1920's women fully dressed is easy because of the boxy, straight silhouettes that were so in style back then!

A fabric belt or sash was worn low on the hips, or there was no belt at all. This helped to create the long, thin, tubular shape that was so desirable during this time period.

KAREN'S QUADRANT METHOD

We will be using my **Quadrant Method** to make drawing easier!

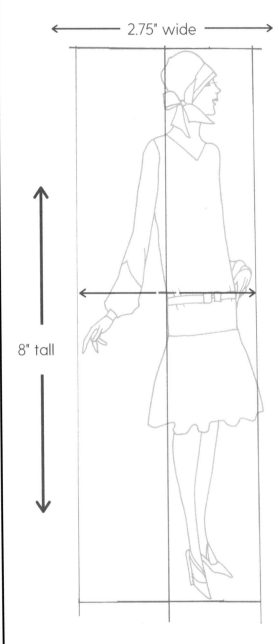

← 2.75" wide →

8" tall

1) Our first objective is to measure out a rectangle around the figure (or any object) to be drawn. Lay a sheet of TRACE PAPER over the reference image and draw a rectangle around it.

Here you can see I have drawn a rectangle (on trace paper) over the model on the previous page.

Take out a ruler and measure the height and width of the girl so you know (roughly) how tall and how wide to make the rectangle. It's about 8" x 2.75".

2) On a **fresh sheet** of drawing paper, lightly sketch a rectangle in the same dimensions. *It's important to sketch our guidelines lightly, so that they can eventually be erased.*

3) Next, sketch a vertical line down the center of your rectangle, and a horizontal line at an obvious reference point. I'm choosing the height of her belt (which happens to be a smidge above half way).

You can choose to create your **Quadrant** guidelines anywhere you like. You don't HAVE to place your first vertical line OR horizontal line down the centers. I feel these are typically helpful starting points. However, in this example, I made my horizontal "center" line at her belt, instead of in the exact center of my rectangle because I felt that location was the most helpful reference point *for me.*

ADDING MORE

Lay your tracing paper over your reference image and add more **Quadrants** as shown below. Sectioning off the reference image in this way will make it easier to draw her.

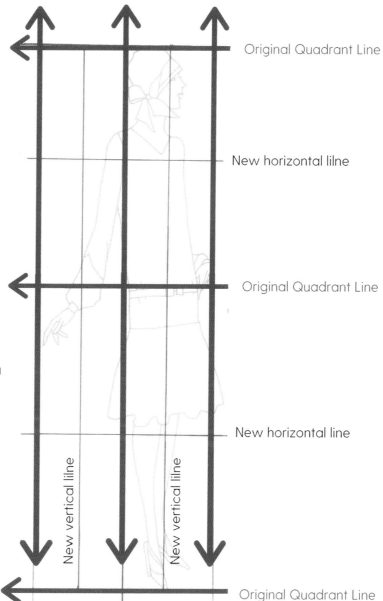

Original Quadrant Line

New horizontal lilne

Original Quadrant Line

New horizontal line

New vertical lilne

New vertical lilne

Original Quadrant Line

Visit
http://bit.ly/quadrantsystem
and see exactly how the
Quadrant method
works to help you draw
anything, even tricky figures!

Then sketch the **Quadrants** from your tracing paper onto your drawing paper. Once your official **Quadrant** has been built, you can begin to draw!

As you begin to sketch in the general outlines of your girl, focus on one **Quadrant** at a time. Slowly proceed through each rectangle, filling in the shapes that you see from that single **Quadrant** before moving on to the next one.

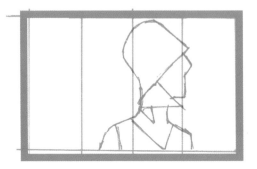

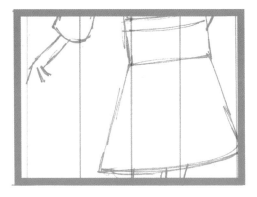

Organizing the figure in this way, makes it super easy to draw because you can focus on only the shapes you see, one **Quadrant** at a time.

You can fill in the **Quadrants** by rows, by columns, or go randomly, one section at a time!

This page shows what it would look like to complete the **Quadrants** by rows.

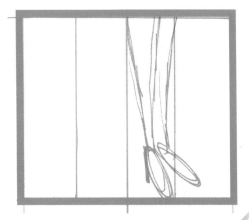

Skip over details at this stage and just focus on the major outlines for now.

Slowly but surely, the **Quadrants** will get filled in...

Just like a PUZZLE!

Once the general outline of the girl has been sketched in, take a second pass over each **Quadrant** and add in the details.

My Quadrants drawn and my finished rough sketch of Reference FIgure in red pen.

Quadrants drawn on trace (placed over the Reference Figure from Page 5).

ADDING MORE

Before we move on, I have to show you something really cool!

With the **Quadrant** method, anytime you need more help drawing a specific area, you can easily add more guidelines in!

Face too tricky? Divide that area into halves again so you have even more guidelines to help you figure out relationships and proportions!

See the three areas where I added additional guidelines (in red)?

Those **Quadrant** regions are now broken down further, so drawing what you see is even easier.

Too many guidelines?

No problem, just erase your way back to the main outline! Another reason to *make sure you are sketching lightly at this stage.*

Once you have all your Quadrants (as many as you need), you're fully ready to draw out the entire fabulous figure onto your own drawing paper and then outline her in with your favorite fineliner.

Once that's finished and your guidelines are erased, you're ready to color her in! Let's Charleston kick to the next page and goooooo!

When it comes to coloring and shading in your drawings, you have so many options of which art supplies to use! I'm a mixed media artist, so I wouldn't feel right if I didn't walk you through at least a few fun options throughout the book. Hopefully the projects and examples will inspire you to try some new techniques or products!

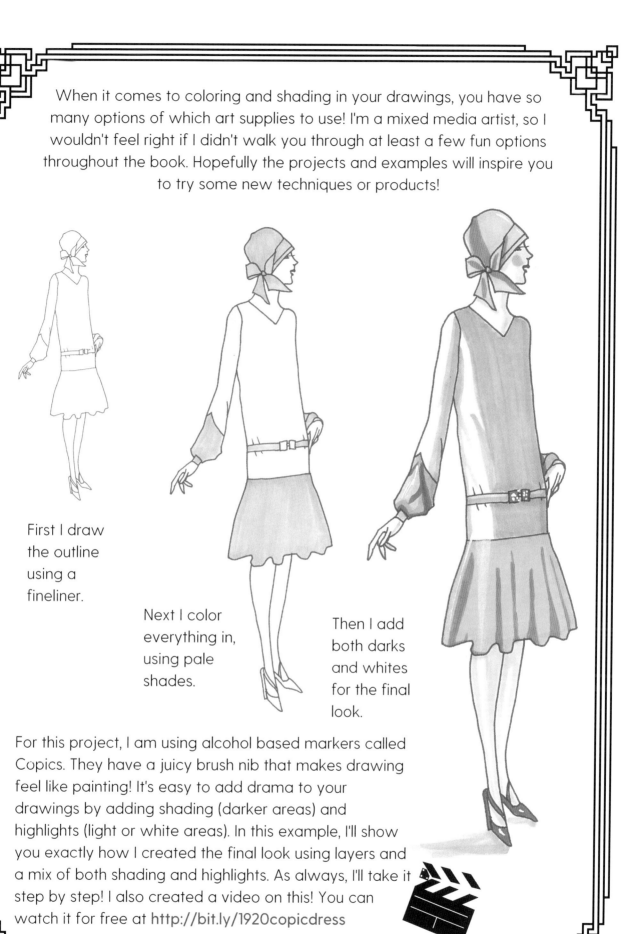

First I draw the outline using a fineliner.

Next I color everything in, using pale shades.

Then I add both darks and whites for the final look.

For this project, I am using alcohol based markers called Copics. They have a juicy brush nib that makes drawing feel like painting! It's easy to add drama to your drawings by adding shading (darker areas) and highlights (light or white areas). In this example, I'll show you exactly how I created the final look using layers and a mix of both shading and highlights. As always, I'll take it step by step! I also created a video on this! You can watch it for free at http://bit.ly/1920copicdress

EASY SHADING

The easy way to create a rich, dimensional drawing is to color using 2-3 shades of every color. So my first step was to pick my colors. I decided on green, grey and peach. My next step was to grab 3 shades of each.

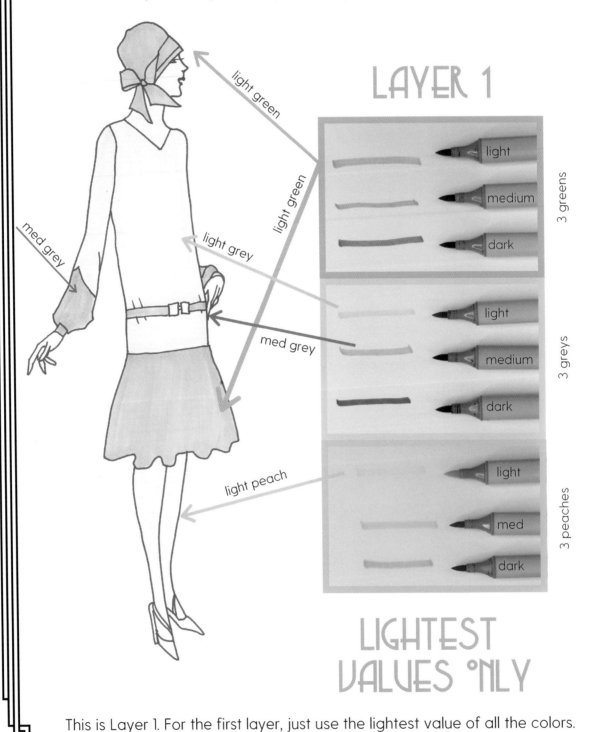

LAYER 1

light green

light green

med grey

light grey

med grey

light peach

3 greens	3 greys	3 peaches
light	light	light
medium	medium	med
dark	dark	dark

LIGHTEST VALUES ONLY

This is Layer 1. For the first layer, just use the lightest value of all the colors.

Layer 2 can be a bit trickier. The best method of creating accurate shadow placement is to use a good reference so you know where to color the shaded parts and where to add highlights .

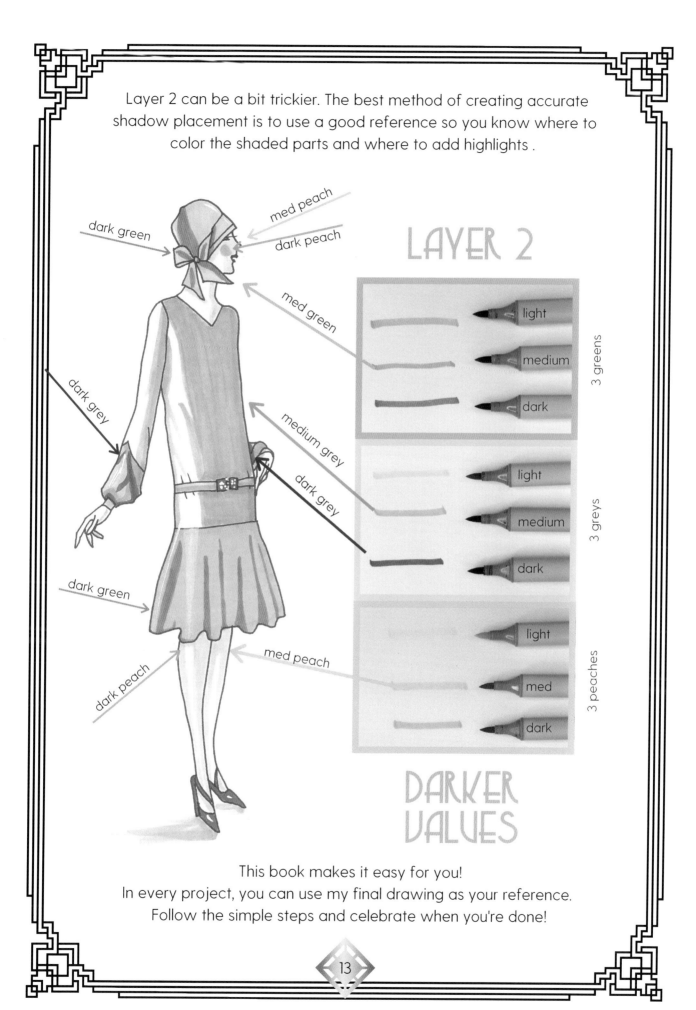

LAYER 2

med peach

dark green

dark peach

med green

3 greens

light

medium

dark

dark grey

medium grey

dark grey

3 greys

light

medium

dark

dark green

med peach

dark peach

3 peaches

light

med

dark

DARKER VALUES

This book makes it easy for you!
In every project, you can use my final drawing as your reference.
Follow the simple steps and celebrate when you're done!

Layer 3 is all about adding white to create highlights. In reality, highlights appear on an object wherever the lightsource is shining the brightest. In drawings, you can use your reference (in this case, my drawings) or you can make up your own lightsource! In this example, light is coming up from the bottom left. This explains why the highlights are along on the left side of her body.

The arrows you see here are all to draw your attention to the highlighted regions!

In fact, they are just as important as the shaded areas for creating depth!

LAYER 3

HIGHLIGHTS ONLY

Note all the light grey from layer 1 peeking through to look like highlights!

My favorites tools to use for highlights are white paint markers from Posca and Sharpie, white colored pencils by Prismacolor (for softer lights), or Pitt Artist Brush pens by Faber-Castell.

Pssst...Can you see the blooper in this drawing? If you said the shadows by her feet were going in the wrong direction, you guessed correctly! Since the light source is coming from the left, the shadows caste should be going to the right. Oops!

MONOCHROMATIC SHADING

If you're short on art supplies, no worries. It's easy to shade even if you only have a single color!

With monochromatic shading you simply keep using darker and darker shades of the same color until you're satisfied with the end result.

I'll show you exactly how this works. Let's go back to the outline. This time, I will be using watercolors.

Add water in different amounts to your palette.

(1) is super watery!

(2) is pretty watery.

(3) has just a little water in it.

(4) is fully saturated watercolor.

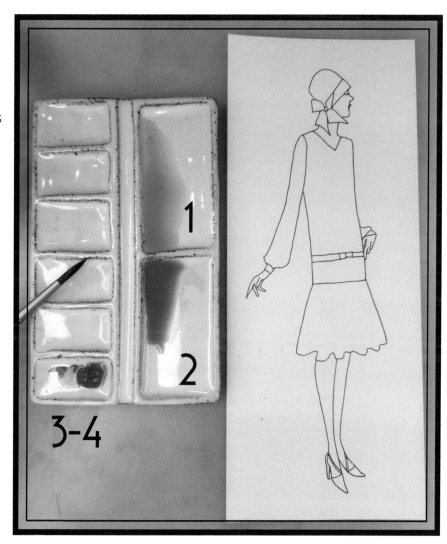

Make sure to ONLY use WATERCOLOR paper when painting. It truly makes a world of difference!!

Just like the previous coloring project, we start with the lightest shades first. That means I'm using my most-watery paint from tray 1. I am also using a very light skin color. This is what the first pass looks like. You can hardly see it. The first shade is so light!

LAYER 1   ## LAYER 2

After you let that layer dry, go back to very specific areas (use the second picture to guide you) and add the paint from the second watery tray. Remember the light source comes from the bottom left so take care to leave those areas open from the second layer!

If you guessed that on Layer 3 we use paint that has even less water (from Tray 3) you'd be 100% correct! Again, the areas you are shading are very specific. That's why references are so important! Whether working from old photos or real life, you need some information about light sources to tell you where to put your light and dark areas. Feel free to let these images guide you!

LAYER 3   LAYER 4

The effects are quite dramatic as you keep going darker and darker with the shades of blue. Notice too, the areas of Layer 4 are used sparingly, just like the white highlights will be.
They both pack a lot of punch, so take care not to overdo either!

It's so important to make sure you know where your light source is coming from (even if it's completely imaginary!!!).

Once you know from what direction the light is coming, be super consistent about your hightlights and place them all along the same side for maximum impact.

HIGHLIGHTS LAYER 5

This little whisper highlight adds a bit more dimension to the hat and keeps it from appearing flat.

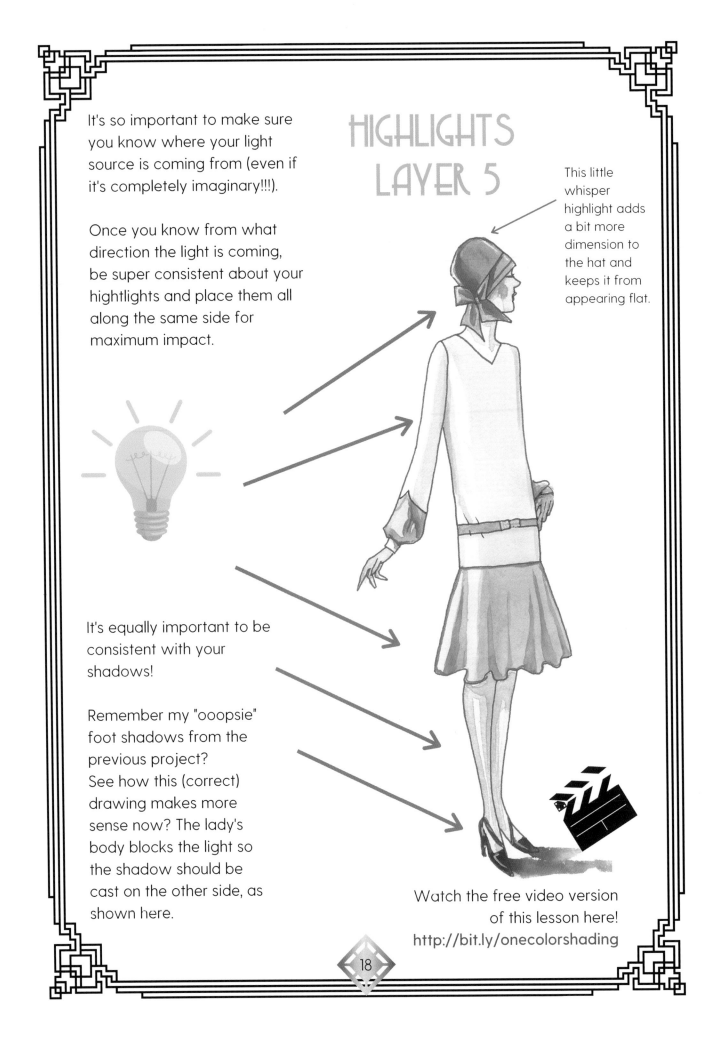

It's equally important to be consistent with your shadows!

Remember my "ooopsie" foot shadows from the previous project? See how this (correct) drawing makes more sense now? The lady's body blocks the light so the shadow should be cast on the other side, as shown here.

Watch the free video version of this lesson here!
http://bit.ly/onecolorshading

FUR C°AT FEVER

Fur coats were all the rage among women during the Jazz Age.

Fur from every animal imaginable (and later on, in faux varieties, for those who couldn't afford the real thing) was used to adorn every conceivable trimpiece of a woman's winter outdoor ensemble.

The fur collar coat, like this one, was what every woman aspired to possess, and most did!

Thankfully, no animals will be hurt in the drawing of these iconic garments, so DRAW WE WILL!

This drawing is based on the illustration gracing the cover of "The Queen" Magazine in 1928.

According to the magazine, the "Striking new model" is wearing "a superior quality nappa leather, richly trimmed with luxurious collar and cuffs of the finest quality North American Skunk."

Ew.

Let's draw!

THE "CHARACTER CONTAINER"

We'll begin this drawing the same way we did the first. You'll need a pencil, a sheet of trace paper and a fresh sheet of drawing paper.

Lay your trace paper over my drawing on the previous page and draw a rectangle around her, as I'm showing here, to the right. This one measures approximately 8" x 2.5".

The vertical guideline is right down the center at 1.25".

For the horizontal guideline in the middle, I am again using the belt (instead of the true center line) as a reference point. That also helps me locate the hands so I can draw them in correctly as well!

I like to refer to this first step of the process as drawing the "Character Container". As if it's our job to build a perfectly fitting little container for our friend (ie. character) in which they will reside for a bit (comfortably, of course!) while we draw them (lest they run away!)!

Next stop, let's divide these Quadrants further.

2 1/2" wide. Centered vertical.

8" tall. Horizontal line at the belt.

DRAW MORE

This is what the **Quadrants** looks like on my tracing paper up to this point.

Should you add more **Quadrants?**

That's totally up to you!

I find that I need at least this many to get started, and oftentimes many more!

The great part about the **Quadrant** method is that after this point the rectangles are so much smaller, you can easily freehand more **Quadrants** in as you need them!

If you haven't watched the video yet on how the **Quadrant** method works, I definitely suggest you take a moment to watch and learn. Besides, it's free!

http://bit.ly/quadrantsystem

Add more | horizontal lines

Add more | horizontal lines

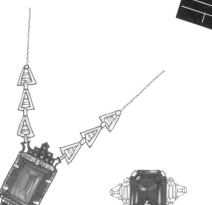

I wonder what jewelry she'd wear?

After you sketch your fabulous fur coated figure, go over your pencil lines with a permanent fineliner.

When I reached the fur sections of my drawing, I replaced my smooth pencil lines with little stipple marks to indicate the appearance of fur, instead of a smoother fabric.

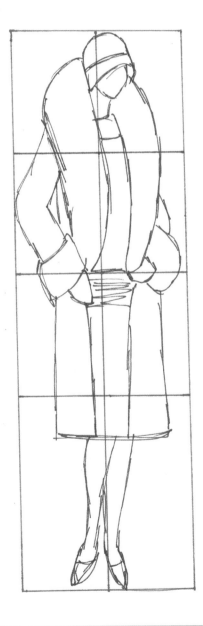

It's so exciting when your drawing gets to this stage! As soon as you're happy, erase those gridlines!!

MARKER BASE LAYER

Choose a base color for each part of your girl. I chose a medium grey for the hat, a medium tan for the coat, a dark brown for the fur trim, and a bright red for the dress and shoes. I'm using Copic markers again. They *can* appear streaky if you don't work quickly. Also applying the marker in small, circular strokes can reduce the look of streaking as well.

little fur marks

little fur marks all over

too slow

better

Creating the look of fur is easy with markers! First, apply a smooth base coat in one solid color. Then choose a slightly darker color and make very short, quick lines over the entire surface of the furry region.

It really is that easy! Turn the page and I'll show you how to accentuate this look even further!

ADDING PENCILS T° THE MIX

Colored pencils are the perfect complement to Copics! They add a lovely bit of texture to the otherwise flat marker appearance. Colored pencils are great at hiding those undesirable marker streaks too!

In this piece I used colored pencils to create shading, interest and texture. I did this by selecting colored pencils that were a shade darker than each of the Copic marker colors I had used to color in the base layer of each section.

To get a more realistic look of fur, I simply added more short strokes but with a darker brown this time. For the leather coat, I added longer streaks of a similar brown to create the look of soft leather. On the dress and hat I added the darker colored pencil in areas to create the look of shadows.

For the final punch though, I added a whisper of paint marker to mark a few individual strands of fur, the lines down the front of her skirt, and on her hat. I cannot resist the bit of drama those create!

FINALLY, A FLAPPER!

All the zazz officially starts here...

SPEAKEASIES AND BOOTLEGGERS!

Pearls for miles, laughter and late nights!

FINGER WAVES AND CUPID BOW LIPS!

BOOZE AND BEAUS!

LUXURIOUS YACHTS!

GLAMOUR AND FURS!

THE CHARLESTON!

Ruffles and shine and Roaring Music!

Skyscrapers!

EXCESS AND SHINE! PARIS! LONDON! OH MY!

Sleek cars and short skirts (almost to the knee!) *GASP*

SET UP YºUR QUADRANTS.

Now that we've done two projects, you know what to do.
Here's a new perspective of the **Quadrant** technique at work. This is my actual studio desk and I, using the system to draw. Your set up should look similar.

First, I'm using my ruler to measure the flapper on the previous page and making the rectangle around her. I'm drawing this on my tracing paper.

Here's a useful shortcut! Instead of redrawing the same rectangle and quadrants onto a separate sheet of paper, if you own a copier or scanner, you can simply make a copy of the **Quadrants** and start to draw on that!

You can see I needed to add a few more **Quadrants** in order to get the details right. No problem. Adding more is easy!
I just free-handed them in as needed (see above, in blue).

RUFFLES AND SHINE!

You can't dive into the Roaring 20's without encountering ruffles everywhere! If we're going to be awesome at drawing ruffles, we better learn how and practice. Let's begin. As always, we'll take it step-by-step!

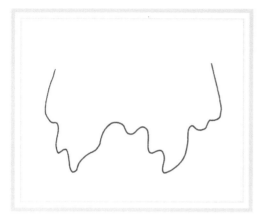

1. Draw a wavy bottom.

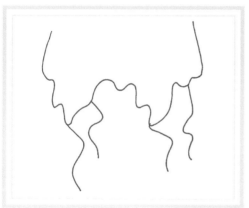

2. Draw loose squiggles.

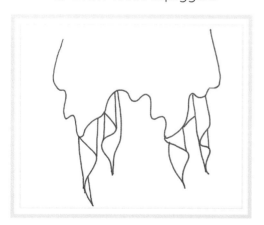

3. Draw vertical lines.

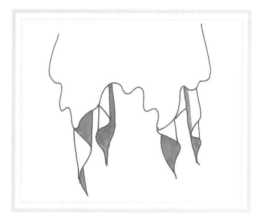

4. Color selected pieces in darkest shade.

5. Color selected in medium shade.

6. Color remaining with light shade.

COLORING TIME!

Now that we understand the mechanics of drawing ruffles, let's color the whole dress! I'm using my Copics again for this project and coloring light to dark (monochromatic style). I hope you'll use what you love most!

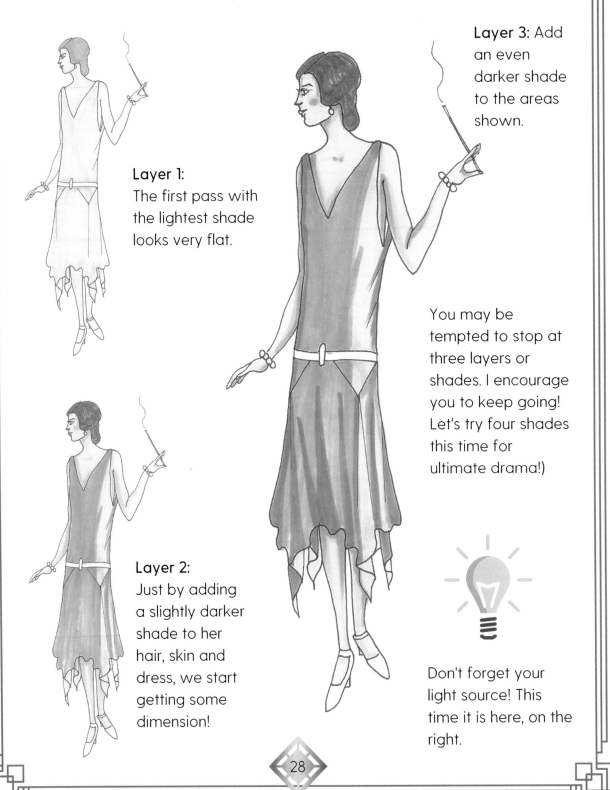

Layer 3: Add an even darker shade to the areas shown.

Layer 1: The first pass with the lightest shade looks very flat.

You may be tempted to stop at three layers or shades. I encourage you to keep going! Let's try four shades this time for ultimate drama!)

Layer 2: Just by adding a slightly darker shade to her hair, skin and dress, we start getting some dimension!

Don't forget your light source! This time it is here, on the right.

The difference is in the details. See the pops of white in the final version? Look closely. What other details do you see that you can add to your version? Details make all the difference. Have FUN with this last step!

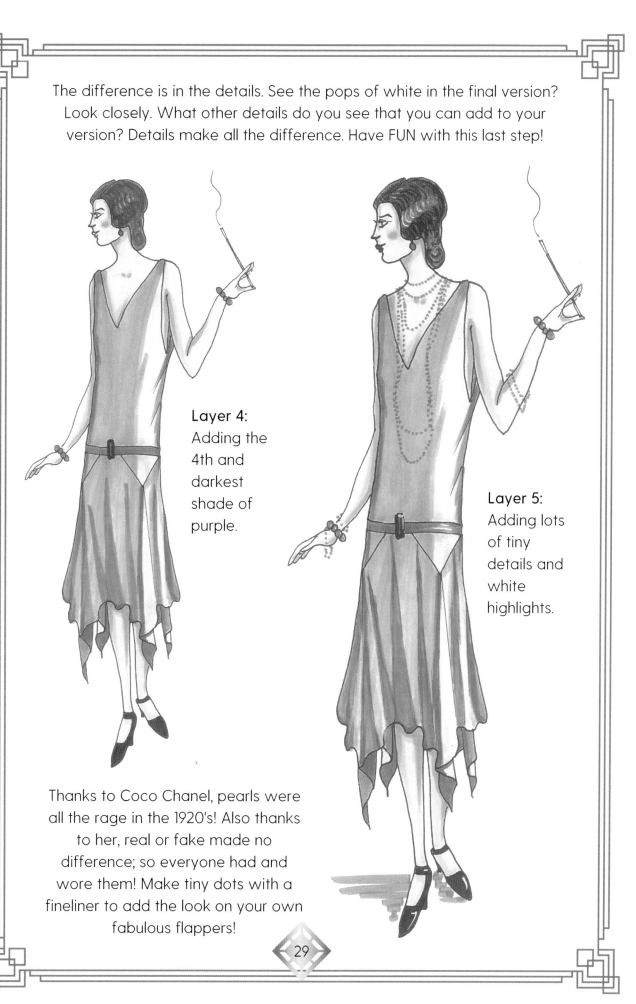

Layer 4:
Adding the 4th and darkest shade of purple.

Layer 5:
Adding lots of tiny details and white highlights.

Thanks to Coco Chanel, pearls were all the rage in the 1920's! Also thanks to her, real or fake made no difference; so everyone had and wore them! Make tiny dots with a fineliner to add the look on your own fabulous flappers!

1929 - ST°CKMARKET AND HEMLINES FALL

As the Stockmarket crashed in 1929, so too did hemlines. Rather than just below the knee, hemlines are almost touching the floor. When I saw this figure on a 1929 McCall's sewing pattern, I knew I had to include her in this book before we segued into 1930's fashion (which is very different from that of the 1920's)! More on that in a few pages. For now, use the **Quadrant** method and this outline to draw her on a separate sheet of paper.

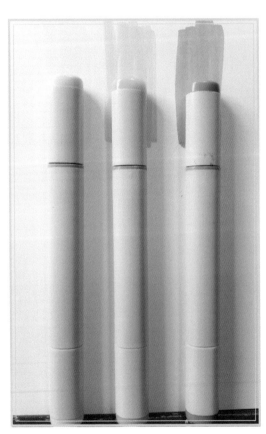

Next, select any color you like. If you can, get a hold of least 3 shades of that one color.

LAYER YOUR COLOR

Layer 1. Apply an all-over light shade to dress, hair and skin.

Layer 2. Apply the medium shade along edges.

Layer 3. Apply the darkest shade to areas under fabric folds.

Layer 4. Apply highlights with white pencil or pen.

http://bit.ly/copicruffles

Watch the video lesson that shows you this exact layering process plus gives you all my best marker tips!

31

Ruffles are complex and can be super confusing. I think it's worth it to look at these a bit more closely. Let's take this step-by-step. This time I'm working in shades of pink. Choose any colors you like!

Draw some lines.

Make squiggles.

Drop vertical lines.

Draw "v" shapes.

Color solid pink.

(Still looks flat)

Add grey to shadowy parts.

(Looks striped - not good)

Adding white to select parts will make some ruffles appear to pop forward!

Everytime you can add more than 2 shades of skin and clothes color, (PLUS a dab of white), you will be creating the illusion of depth, dimension and enhance the overall fashion drama!

Enhance edges that move away from you with darker shades of the dress color + grey.

WATERC°L°R ... MARKERS ?

Did you know that there are some markers that can act like watercolors? The best part? All you need is one of these magical markers, and a little water, and you can make magic happen too! Here I am using watercolor marker in green, by Winsor-Newton. You color with them just like regular markers, then add water to make the ink flow! Make sure that you **ONLY use watercolor paper** when giving this a try, or it won't work properly.

First I gently colored in only the places you see here. These markers are SO reactive, a little ink goes a long way!

Then I took a slightly damp watercolor brush and coaxed the pigment where I wanted it to go!

I added a second layer of marker under the folds of the ruffles to make them darker (like in the previous exercise), added a touch more water to blend it in, and done!

THE NEW DECADE

After the market crash of 1929, money wasn't the only change in society. The new decade brought a huge change to women's fashion as well. Hemlines hit the floor once again and waist lines traveled quickly, all the way back up to the waist! In sharp contrast to the tubular, low waisted, boyish style of the roaring 20's, the 1930's brought with it long and lean elegance in tight gowns that hugged and accentuated every curve punctuated by a dramatic flare down below the ankles.

No curves (bum or bust!)

Low or no waist

Almost to knee

Dresses were long and lean

Tight belts at the waist

Accentuated the figure

Long and flared

Even dogs became long and lean in the 30's. Like this Borzoi!

Learn to draw lots of dogs in Vol. 2!

1920'S SILHOUETTE

1930'S SILHOUETTE

30'S EVENING GOWN

By now you know exactly how to get started.

This is your reference sketch.

First, get out your trace paper and ruler. Next, measure out the rectangle around this swanky lady!

Then establish your **Quadrants**. Will you have a lot? A few? The choice is up to you!

Next, do your best to draw the same exact **Quadrants** that you drew on your trace, onto your drawing paper.

Lastly, draw this girl on your drawing paper using **Quadrants** to help you see where things go!

Need coloring help?

I got you.

Just turn the page!

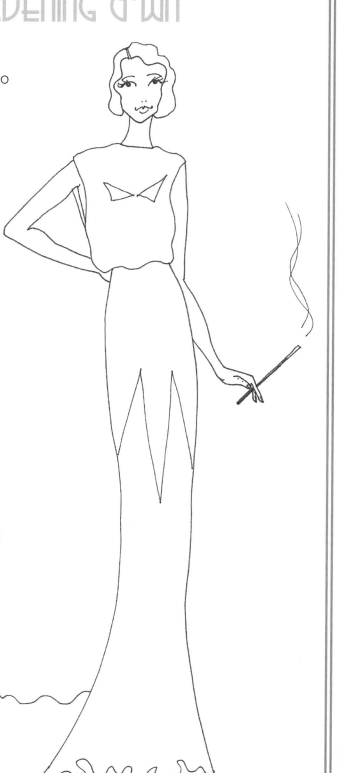

Step 1.

Add a layer of Copics going horizontally across the dress. Use the lightest shade here.

The horizontal brush strokes give the appearance of dimension. See how it already looks like she is curving from one side of her body to the other?

Step 2.

Use a darker shade of pink to make patterns (or the illusion of "gathers") in the top of her dress as shown.

Then color the edges of her dress in long vertical strokes at the edges and towards the bottom as it flares out the ends.

Add more on the train.

HELPFUL TRICKS

To get the look of fabric (and to eliminate those pesky marker streaks), get two shades of pink colored pencils that are roughly the same color as the markers you used for Steps 1 and 2.

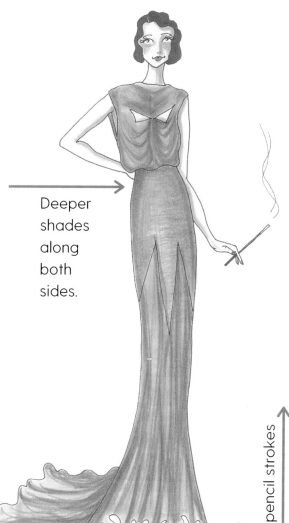

Deeper shades along both sides.

Step 3.
Alternating between the two colored pencils, color lightly in BOTH directions, just as we did with the markers.

Step 4.
Add more of the darker colored pencil towards the edges to create more dimension.

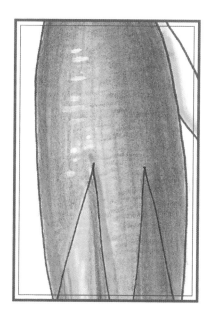

pencil strokes

pencil strokes

You can see the marker streaks slowly start to disappear as you add the pencil.

Step 5.

Go back in with the markers one more time. Run the darker Copic color around the gown (and leaving it lighter in the middle). This creates the appearance of her figure being truly round and three dimensional. Keep layering until you're happy!

Step 6.

Add white highlights when you're through. I repeated the pink in her cheeks and lips to match. I think a true 1930's girl would approve!

THE SIMPLE BLACK DRESS

The simple black dress has had it's version in all decades throughout female fashion history. No version is as sexy or dramatic as this elegant 1930's number!

The design is simple to draw and something that is fun to practice in lots of different shades of color! Use the large outline here to build the rectangle and **Quadrants** onto your own paper.

SHADES °F GREY.

Since there are no shades of black, grey is your next best option! Start off slowly when drawing black dresses. Begin with medium shades of grey and slowly build up color.

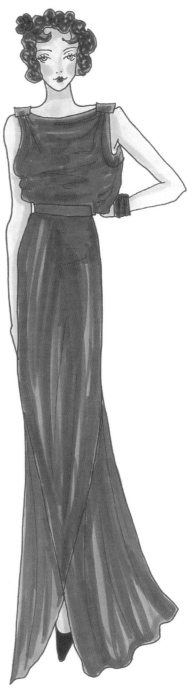

Step 1. Use a shade of medium grey for the dress, a light shade of skin tone for the ski and a light shade of brown for the hair.

Step 2.
Add a darker shade of grey (all over) for the dress. You can leave gaps to allow the first, lighter shade to show through.

Add a slightly darker shade for the skin in just a few places like under the chin, along the hairline, on the cheeks, and along the insides of the arms.

Add a darker shade to the hair.

Step 1.

Step 2.

Step 3.

Step 4.

Step 5.

Add the first
whisper of
black.

Not dark enough but afraid
to add more black because
you'll lose all definition? Opt
for some darker shades of
grey instead.

Add subtle OR not-so-subtle
hightlights!

PRACTICE & PLAY T° IMPR°VE!

The best way to get better at drawing and coloring is to PLAY! Instead of doing each project in this book once, consider having FUN and doing one drawing a couple of times to see what happens! Try variations, try colors, try new skin tones, experiment with different highlights. Just HAVE FUN! You'll learn more by playing than you will by any other means.

SKIN TONES ALL WORK THE SAME.

Choosing different skin tones is easy! Think of skin tones the same way you'd think of a greyscale: simply a continuum of color (or a series of shades going from light to dark). To depict lovely shaded skin in any tone, simply move up or down the skin tone scale as desired! Like shading anything, pick out 2 or 3 shades to add dimension!

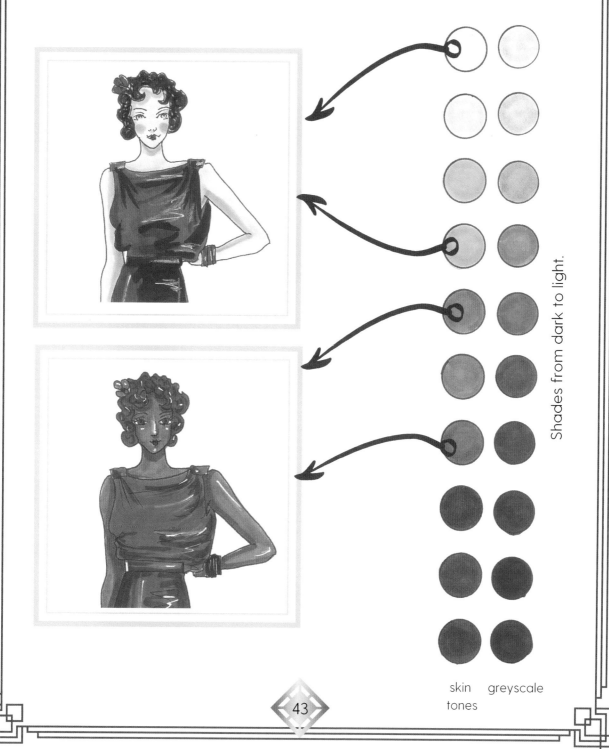

Shades from dark to light.

skin tones   greyscale

SHADING SKIN TONES

This easy shading figure method is used for every person, male or female, and for evey shade and color of skin too!

First, put down the lightest shade (wherever that may be on the skin tone continuum).

Second, shade around the hairline. More specifically, choose a slightly darker shade, and run a line around the hairline. In this case, it almost encompasses the whole face. That's okay!

Plenty of shading under the chin, always.

If no nose bridge is drawn, add a line of shading to one side.

If you're assuming the lightsource is coming straight at a person, or even from the side, the area closest to the body SHOULD be in shadow. So run a layer of shading here.

Add shading to areas facing AWAY from the sun or a perceived light source.

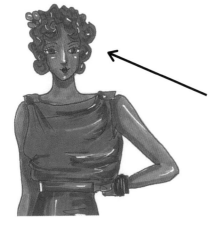

There's no reason you can't pop beautiful highlights on skin too! Dark skin affords a wonderful opportunity to add little pops of white. You can put highlights on the nose bridge, cheeks, pupil, chin, and swipes in the hair, down arms and across fabric! So fun!

1930's OUTERWEAR

It seems that women (and men!) had appetites for fur that did not diminish in the new decade. Luckily, Coco Chanel made faux fur as fashionable as real fur, so everyone got to own their dream winter coat!

Just like 1930's evening and day wear, coats were just as long, lean and gorgeous! This particular sewing design was available with or without the fur trim! You learned how to render fur a few figures back...want to give it another go? Or do you prefer the sleek cut without all the fluffy-fur-in-your-face version as much as I do?

Speaking of fur...

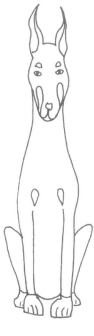

And more in Vol. 2!

D°GGIE DETAILS

The Art Deco era favored dogs that were long and lean. Think Greyhound, Borzoi and Great Dane! I thought a Doberman paired well with our lady!

Step 1.
Determine how tall your dog will be and then divide that height into thirds.

Step 2.
Draw these oval shapes in each section.

Step 3.
Refine the shapes of the ears and head. Add leg lines and paws.

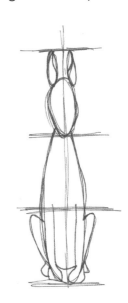

Step 5.
Outline with fineliner.

Step 4.
Add details.

Step 6.
Color as desired!

PURE INK-SPIRATION

Are you ready for something new? We've covered markers, watercolors, watercolor markers and some colored pencil work so far. But now I'm going to introduce you to my absolute newest obsession:
painting with fountain pen inks.

Technically, you're not supposed to paint with these inks at all. You fill your fountain pens with the ink and write with them like a normal person.
I am not a normal person.

Remember: Only use on watercolor paper!

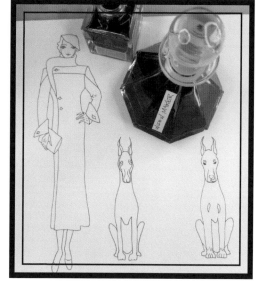

I love Fabriano Hot Pressed!

You paint with inks the same way you paint with watercolor. You can paint with them undiluted as you see I'm doing here, or you can water them down.

My favorite way to paint is to dip a watercolor brush straight into my fancy container of ink and put it right to paper! I chose this color for this project for the name alone: Widow Maker. And yes, it is blood red! It would take 6 coats of watercolor to create this depth of color! Yum! With ink, you get it in ONE.

Want to learn more about painting with Fountain Pen Ink? Just visit this link and I'll explain everything! http://bit.ly/fountainpeninklove

FINAL TOUCHES

Ink requires minimal time and effort and produces maximum effect! LOVE it! I hope you'll try it and love it too.

I've only had to use a single layer of red, nude, black and brown ink to color the lady entirely!

The Doberman was colored in using only one layer of black and brown ink.

To finish the painting all I did was add a little colored pencil (in grey) in places around her coat and dabs of a white gel pen here and there. (I did add cheeks, eye and lip-color using a pat of watercolor marker too).

S° EASY!

MAKE-UP

AND HAIR

As already mentioned, the Art Deco period marked the beginning of women's fierce independence. Therefore, it is no coincidence that this was the first time in history that women decided to chop all their hair off!

The first bob was recorded in 1915 by Irene Castle (a glamorous ballroom dancer) who cut her hair for purely practical reasons! She was having an appendectomy and didn't want to have to do her hair while in the hospital!

At first the move to cut hair that short was so shocking that barbers refused to do it!

Even Coco Chanel had to take matters into her own hands when her distressed maid refused to do the honors. She grabbed the kitchen shears and did it herself!

The 1920's also marked the first time in history that make-up was worn by women other than showgirls and prostitutes. So exciting!

From the Eton, the Marcel and Finger Wave hairstyles, to cupid-bow lips and kohl eyeliner (inspired by King Tut himself!), we now have some exciting things to draw!

MORE EYE-DEAS!

You can leave off the lower lid but still have a few sparse lower lashes to "hint" that it's still there!

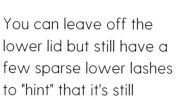

Eyebrow plucking was definitely the "in" move in the 1930's. The thinner (and then drawn in longer) the better!

You can include a small dash for the tear duct...or not!

Kohl eyeshadow and cake mascara make their debuts in this era!

Feel free to have eyes looking off to the side! It's boring to always have them looking straight on!

If you accidently color the entire pupil in, you can always add the little twinkle back in with a white gel pen!

You can draw large lids that connect to the eyes.

Or skip the upper lids entirely!

EYES

NOSES

Before we get to drawing the make-up and full face, let's draw the eyes, step-by-step.

Noses are easier than you think!

Step 1. Draw top lids

Step 1. Draw two slanted ovals

Step 2. Draw irises. (note: these are **not** full circles, rather half circles).

Step 2. Draw parenthesis around your ovals.

Step 3. Thicken top lid. Add pupils.

Leave a white sparkle!

Step 3. Draw a quick swipe off to to one side or the other.

Step 4. Add lids and eyebrows.

Step 5. Add lashes. A few or a lot!

Step 4. Draw a quick swipe again.

NOTE the directionality of the lashes. Lashes curve at the edges of the eyes and switch directions in the middle.

Noses are made up of the shadows around them. This last little swipe (which indicates the ball of the nose), is also fun but completely optional.

DRAWING EYE MAKE-UP

King Tut's tomb was discovered in 1922 and it is no coincidence that wearing kohl eyeliner became all the rage after that! As I said, this marked the first time in history that it was socially acceptable for women OTHER than streetwalkers and stage performers to apply heavy make-up (that's a big deal!). Black grease pencil was smudged all around the eyes to create a deep-set eye effect. Cake mascara was applied generously to create long, bold lashes! I'm using watercolor markers here but use whatever you like!

Step 1. Draw 3 squished ovals.
(Middle ensures proper spacing)

Step 2. Refine eye shapes.

Step 3. Add thin wet line along bottom. Draw irises and pupils.

Step 4. Outline the eyes with black watercolor marker. Add desired color to iris and add water to blend.

Step 5. Drag a wet paint brush (with water) and run it all around the eyes. Be sure to leave the middle of the upper eyelid lighter than the rest.

 Step 6. Draw thin eyebrows sloping down. Add lashes and white highlights with a paint pen. Need some extra drawing help? Watch the video lesson that accompanies this project!
http://bit.ly/1920eyes

LIPS

The "cupid's bow" mouth was all the rage and was drawn carefully (sometimes with the use of a stencil!) within the natural outline of the lips.

 Step 1. Draw a "v"

 Step 2. Draw sloped lines to either side.

 Step 3 Connect ends. Add short line below.

 Step 4. Connect ends. to top lip.

Step 5. Color and add pops of white highlights!

CHEEKS

Before rouge was added, women first applied LOTS of very white powder to their whole face, often shades lighter than their real skin shade. Only then was blush applied in circles on the apples of the cheeks. The effect was a very rounded face. This is very different than the sharp contouring that's so fashionable today!

THEN   54   NOW

THE CLASSIC FLAPPER L°°K

Let's draw a close-up face that represents the "classic" 1920's look!
We will go over hair and make-up trends as we draw!

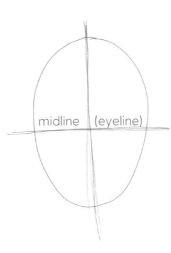

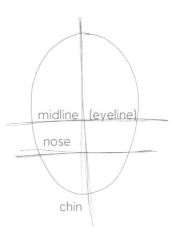

Step 1. Draw an oval.

Step 2. Draw a horizontal and vertical line across the center.

Step 3. Draw a horizontal halfway between the midline and chin.

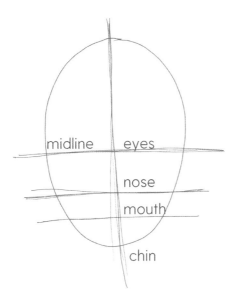

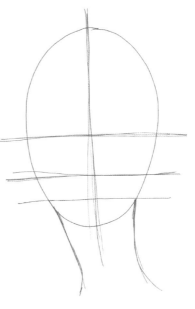

Step 4. Draw a horizontal halfway between the nose line and chin.

Step 5. Draw two lines for the neck.

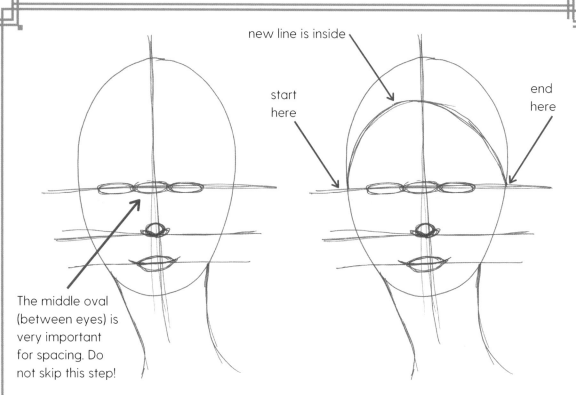

new line is inside

start
here

end
here

The middle oval
(between eyes) is
very important
for spacing. Do
not skip this step!

Step 6. Draw ovals where the features will go.

Step 7. Add a second line on the head (inside the head line, starting from the eyeline).

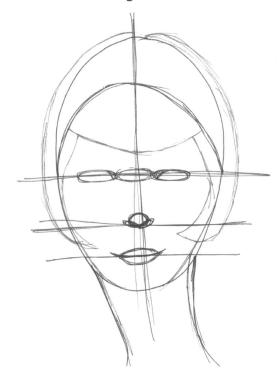

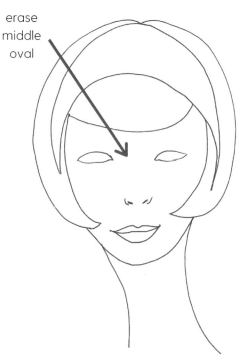

erase
middle
oval

Step 8. Define the face, neck and eyes a bit more (see red). Add hair.

Step 9. Outline everything with a fineliner. Erase guidelines.

Step 10. Add eye details. Now is the best time to make changes (before we add color!).

Step 11. Want to add a flower to her headband? Erase her bottom eye line? Add a mole? Different bangs? Cupid-bow lips? This is step to do it!

Step 12. Add a light base coat to all areas. I'm using Copics markers.

Step 13. Add one shade darker to checks, around eyes, under neck.

Step 14. Add 2 shades of grey around eyes. The darker shade goes closest to the eye.

Step 15. Add even darker shades to everything.

Step 15. Add Indigo or Grey colored pencil to deepen shaded areas around eyes, face and neck if desired.

Step 16. Add lashes and pops of highlights to the eyes and on lips!

S° MANY B°BS!

After much research, I was very much blown away by the overwhelming number of bob hairstyles there were! Here are just SOME of them!

BRUSHBACK

dutch boy

FR!ZZ

CHARLESTON

WINDSWEPT

ETON CROP

SHINGLE

moana

THE POODLE

ORCH!D BOB

EGYPTIAN

BUT REALLY JUST 2...OR 4.

Thankfully I ran across a great website, **vintagedancer.com**, that was able to sum the myriad of styles up very succinctly by saying, *"Bob cuts came in different styles with funny names...but there were only two main styles. Short and curly or short and straight. Most bobs hovered around the earlobe length with a center or deep off-center part."* I will add here that both of these styles can either include bangs...or not. So I suppose that makes 4 styles. Still, I feel better!

That is a number we can play around with and draw easily in this book. This is the point in our drawings in which we can play!

Original head oval (dashed line).

Original head oval (dashed line).

Based on that description, this would be the **straight** style with a **middle** part, **with** bangs.

Same **straight** style with **middle** part and **no** bangs. Easy! We got this!

Play with different headbands and hairstyle to get the 20's look you're going for! After you draw the hair shape (so right after this step) you can erase your head oval and now begin coloring your hairstyle in the medium of your choice!

MORE STRAIGHT BOBS

But before we start coloring, let's just go over the final styles. There's only a few!

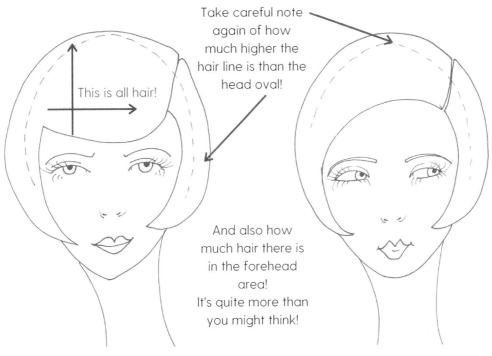

Take careful note again of how much higher the hair line is than the head oval!

This is all hair!

And also how much hair there is in the forehead area!
It's quite more than you might think!

This is how to draw the **straight style** with **bangs** and **far side part**.

This is how to draw the **straight style** with **no bangs** and **far side part**.

This is a photo of my paternal grandmother in 1926. She is sporting the straight bob, no bangs, side part, just like the top right drawing!

This is a photo of my maternal grandmother. She is sporting the curvy bob, no bangs, side part in early 30's.

I used to think they looked funny and old-fashioned. Now I have such a deep appreciation of just how trendy they were!

CURLY HAIR BOBS

And remember, after you draw the
hair shape, you're ready for color!

As always, I'm
leaving the head
oval dashed in red
so you can
appreciate the
volume that real
hair has!

This is how to draw the curly **style**
with **bangs** and **middle part**.

This is how to draw the curly **style**
with **no bangs** and **middle part**.

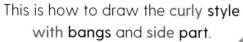

This is how to draw the curly **style**
with **bangs** and **side part**.

This is how to draw the curly **style**
with **no bangs** and **side part**.

DISCTINCTIVE WAVES

Women in the Art Deco period did not mess around when it came to their curls! The Finger Wave was, by far, the most popular hair curl design!

Notice the distinct "S" shape waves in these **Finger Waves.**

The **Eton Curl is** a tight, singular curl placed directly against the face. It was a pretty way to break up an otherwise very short, boy-style bob.

Created by setting the hair into waves using the fingers to create "S" shapes using a combination of fingers, pins and gels/lotions to hold it in place until it dried. It was always worn close to the head.

The popular **Marcel wave** was a tighter version of the finger wave and made possible by a curling-iron heating tool invented by Francois Marcel in the early 1900's.

DRAWING WAVES IN PROFILE

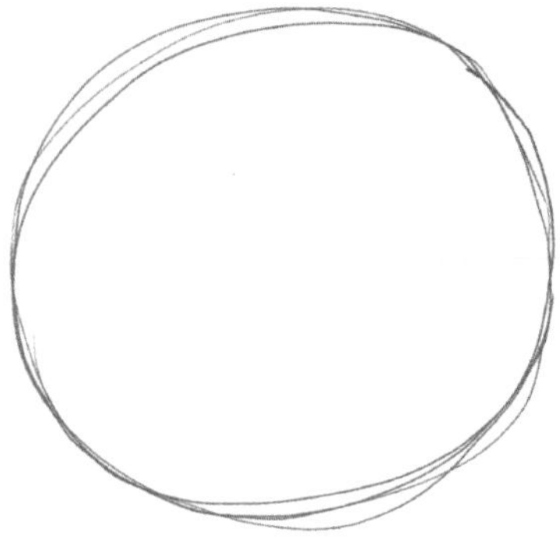

Step 1. Draw a circle.

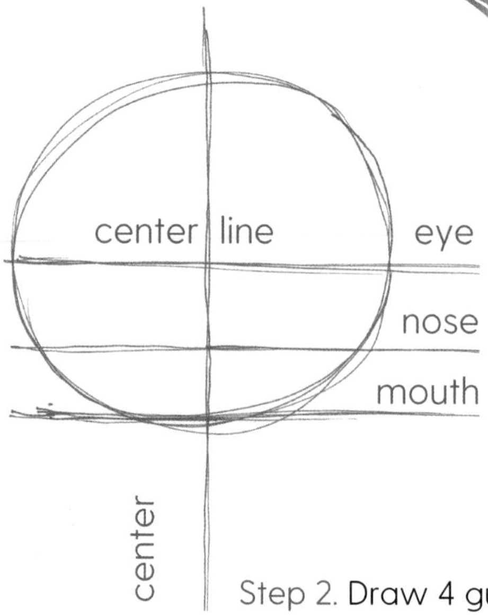

center line   eye

nose

mouth

center

Step 2. Draw 4 guidelines.

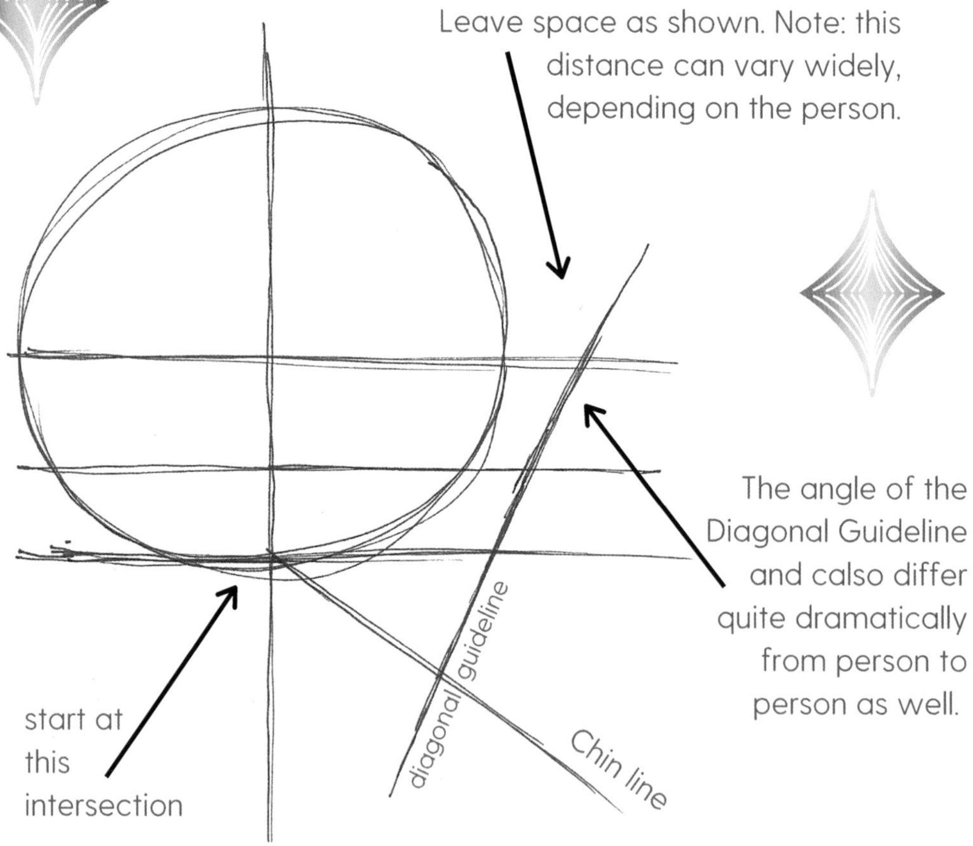

Leave space as shown. Note: this distance can vary widely, depending on the person.

The angle of the Diagonal Guideline and calso differ quite dramatically from person to person as well.

diagonal guideline

Chin line

start at this intersection

Step 3. Add 2 guidelines as shown.

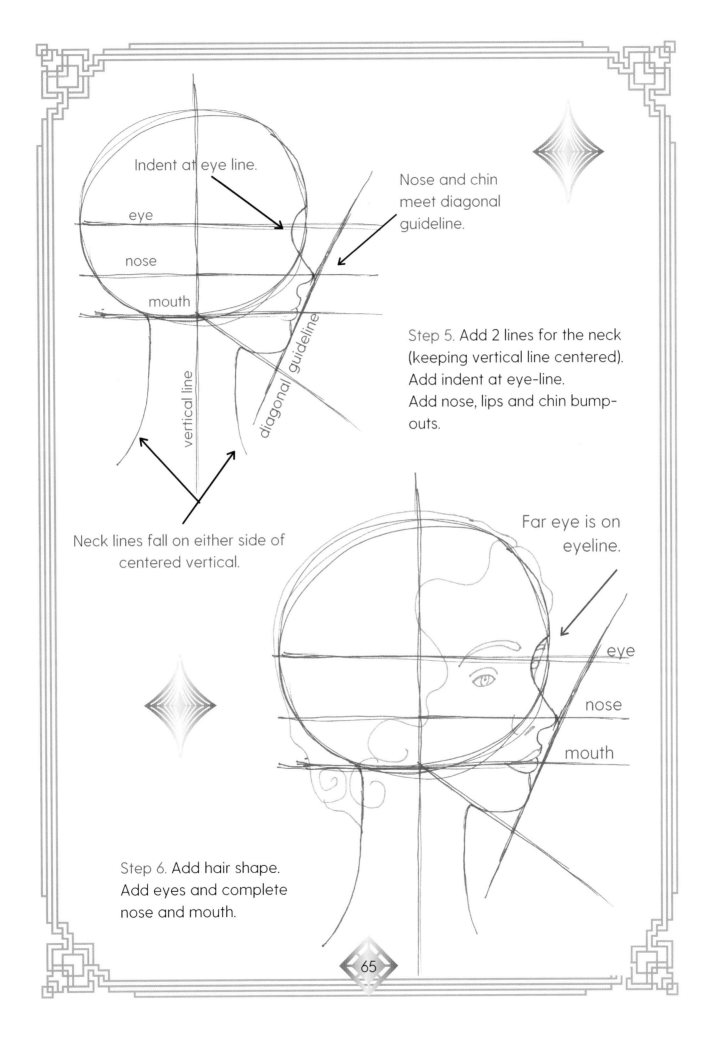

Indent at eye line.

eye

nose

mouth

vertical line

diagonal guideline

Nose and chin meet diagonal guideline.

Step 5. Add 2 lines for the neck (keeping vertical line centered).
Add indent at eye-line.
Add nose, lips and chin bump-outs.

Neck lines fall on either side of centered vertical.

Far eye is on eyeline.

eye

nose

mouth

Step 6. Add hair shape.
Add eyes and complete nose and mouth.

DRAWING FINGER WAVES

Step 7. Draw outline with fineliner. Erase guidelines.

Step 8. Start with lightest color. Draw short strokes in the direction of alternating "C" shapes.

Step 9. Add a darker shade. Draw a series of smaller size "C"s in alternating directions.

Step 10. Add a 3rd, darker shade. Repeat the same "C" drawing process.

KEEP LAYERING TH°SE "C"S

Add white
pencil between
the waves.

Step 11. Add 4th darkest shade.
of marker.

Step 12. Add white colored
pencils to highlighted places.

Step 13. Go over the entire head
with the first/lightest marker color
to blend all the colors together.

Continue on to the next page so
we can color her face!

FACE SHADING

Step 14. Add an all over base coat of any skin tone.

Step 15. Add a slightly darker shade to the areas shown.

Step 16. Add a 3rd and final dark shade around the eyes, along the nose, along the hairline and under the chin. Add white highlights.

Congratulate yourself on a job well done! This is a very difficult project!

HATS,
SH°ES
AND
ACCESS°RIES

While hair locks were short, decor over them was EVERYTHING!

Beads, felt, feathers, headbands and FUN!

Long pearls, dangly earrings and chunky bracelets were "in" and worn by everyone!

Thanks to faux being readily available and made socially acceptable by the likes of Coco Chanel, accessorizing was something that every woman could partake in!

And hats! We cannot discuss Art Deco without mentioning (and drawing and coloring) the many hats of the day – the most popular by far being the cloche hat.

Get your pencils ready and let's begin!

THE CL°CHE

The cloche hat was THE hat for women to wear during the Art Deco period. The short brim was often cut so low that a women had to raise her chin and lower her eyes to see properly! This, of course, gave her an air of dignity and even arrogance (*oh la la!*).

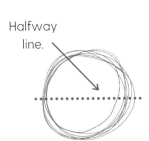

Halfway line.

Step 1. Draw a circle

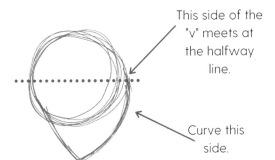

This side of the "v" meets at the halfway line.

Curve this side.

Step 2. Add a "v".

Outline hat.

Step 3. Add a neck.

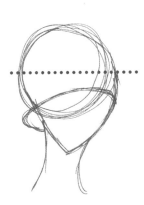

Step 4. Add a curved line as shown.

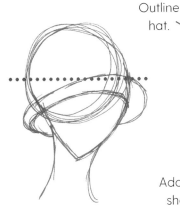

Step 5. Add a second curved line.

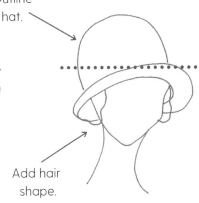

Add hair shape.

Step 6. Erase extraneous lines.

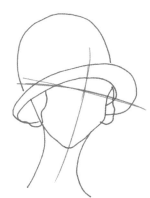

Step 7. Draw eyeline and centerline.

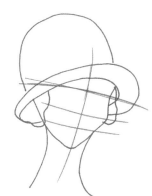

Step 8. Add nose and mouth line.

Step 9. Sketch features.

THE CLOCHE CONTINUED...

Even as simple as the cloche hat was, it had a huge effect on many aspects of fashion for women - from colors, to styles, to haircuts! The popular Eton and Bob haircut paired beautifully with these hats which were often custom made to fit a woman's head (and haircut!).

I know that red eye looks silly but keeping that space is very important!

Step 10. Erase face guidelines. Make sure your eyes have an entire "eye-width" between them!

Step 11. Add details to the facial features.

Step 12. Color with your favorite mediums! I'm using Copics.

Step 13. Note the face/hat shading and hair details!

ADD EMBELLISHMENTS

Flowers, beads, bows, ribbons, appliques and brooches were all easy accessories which could be added, on a whim, to match a particular mood, season, or outfit! Now that you can draw a simple cloche, let's practice adding some embellishments to them!

Now that you can draw this one simple face and hat shape, it's easy to repeat the drawing. Change up the hair, skin color, and embellishments, of course!

SEEK INSPIRATION

You can Google images of Art Deco fashion and cloche hats! Then see if you can draw what you see!

WHAT'S NEXT?

Now that you know the steps to drawing the head and some basic hat forms, you can draw almost any style you like! Take time and a little extra effort to add layers to your drawings, no matter how simple your subject seems to be. Taking care to add shading and details really makes a big (and FUN) impact!

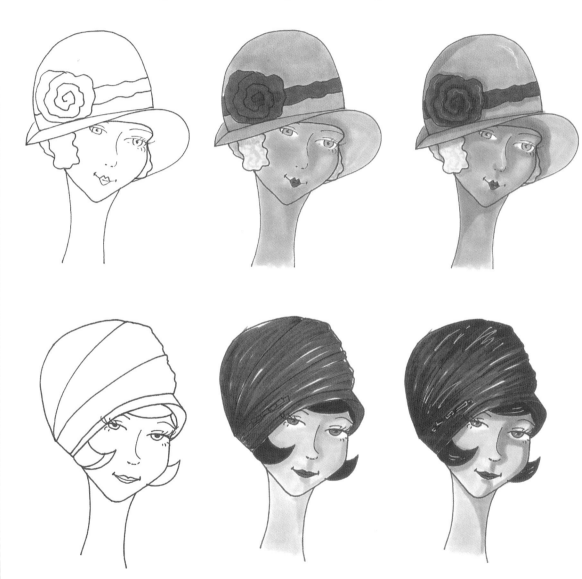

If you go onto Pinterest or Google and do a search for 1920's cloche hats you will see a positively *dizzying* array of hats that you can draw and color! Different fun colors, shapes, bling, short brims, wide brims, brimless, flowers, felt, beads and bows, so much fun! If you're looking for endless inspiration you are truly only a click or two away!

BERETS & TURBANS

Besides the cloche, there were SO many other fabulous hat designs during this era! First we will learn to draw a beret on a forward facing woman.

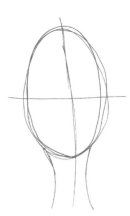

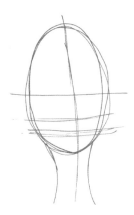

Step 1. Draw an oval

Step 2. Draw a vertical and horizontal line down and across the middle.

Step 3. Draw 2 more horizontal lines. They don't have to be exact. All humans are a bit differently proportioned!

There should be enough space between the eyes for a 3rd eye!

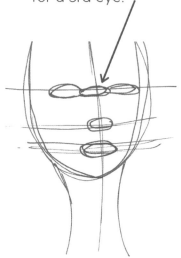

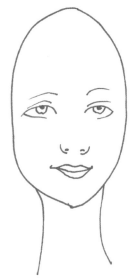

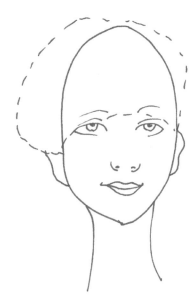

Step 4. Lightly sketch ovals which will indicate the placement of the eyes, nose and mouth.

Step 5. Refine the facial features using simple shapes.

Step 6. Plan how the hat will sit on top of the head. Look how voluminous the head really is!

Step 7. Outline your head and hat with a fineliner pen. Erase pencil marks.

Step 8. Color beret as desired!

Step 9. Add more shading and white highlights.

Now that you know the steps of the head, you can draw a face again. This time change it up! Add a flower, some earrings, a necklace....a mole!

BRIMLESS!

It seemed the cloche hat could be whipped up into thousands of different styles, colors and fabrics. Some were even brimless and hugged the bob so closely, it's no wonder women had no choice but to cut their hair off just to be able to fit their heads into their favorite hats! Let's draw another pretty profile!

Step 1. Draw a circle.

Step 3. Draw a curved line straddling the eye line.

Step 2. Draw a line across the center. That's the eyeline.

Step 4. Draw 2 lines here and here.

Step 5. Fill in the features as shown.

Step 6. Add neck from the intersection of lines.

I ended up reducing the size of the back of the head for this drawing, although it is still anatomically accurate to have that big circle for the head in profile view! I trimmed mine for aesthetic purposes. As an artist, isn't it lovely to be able to do what you like?

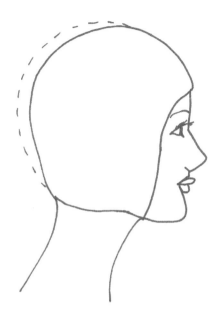

Step 7. With fineliner, outline the face and features. Erase guidelines.

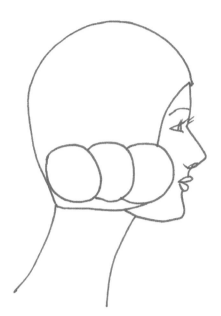

Step 8. Draw circles for decoration.

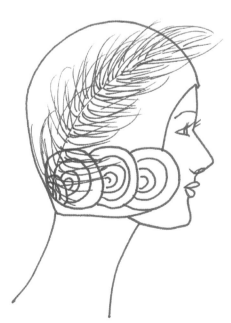

Step 9. Draw lots of loose, lines for the feather and more circles.

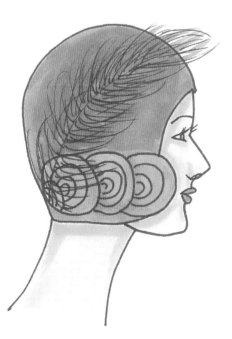

Step 10. Color as desired!

Check out high budget TV shows and movies like Downton Abbey, Peaky Blinders and The Great Gatsby for unbelievably awesome Art Deco Fashion ideas and further inspiration!!

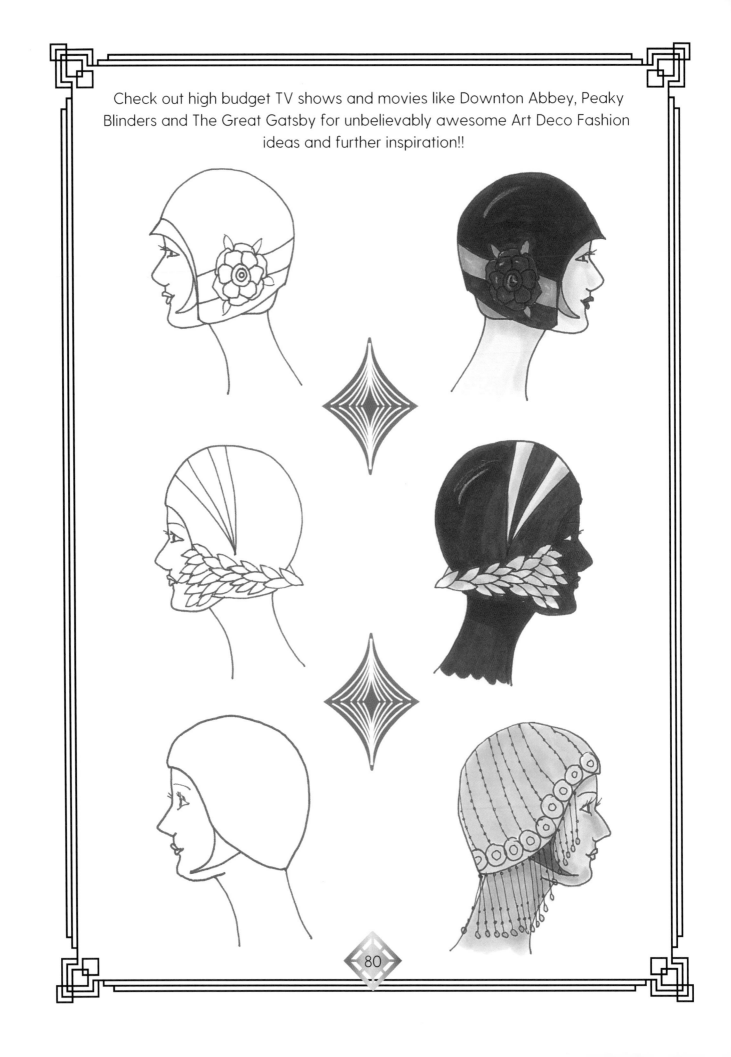

WIDE BRIMMED HATS

Follow the simple steps, one line at a time as show, below, to create this gorgeous head and hat combination!

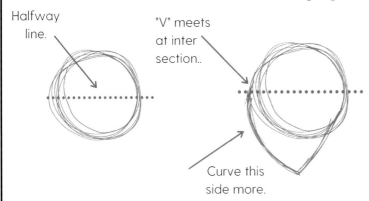

Halfway line.

"V" meets at inter section..

Curve this side more.

Step 1. Draw a circle

Step 2. Add a "v".

Step 3. Add a neck.

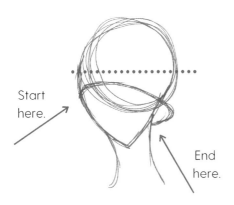

Start here.

End here.

Step 4. Add a curved line as shown.

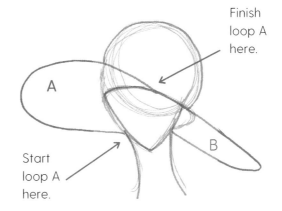

Finish loop A here.

A

Start loop A here.

B

Step 5. Add 2 Loops. Loop A and B.

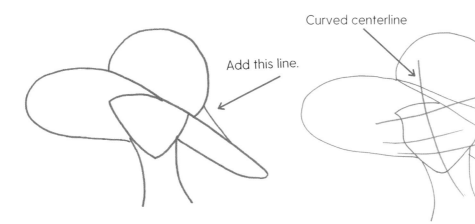

Add this line.

Curved centerline

eyes
nose
mouth

Step 6. Add small line. Erase extraneous lines.

Step 7. Add face guidelines as shown.

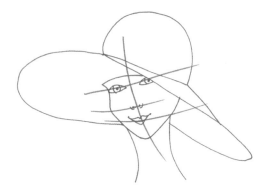

Step 8. Draw in features.

Step 9. Erase guidelines.
Draw the details.

Step 10. Color. Add shading &
white hightlights!

Step 11. Have fun coming up with new
designs based on old photos, Pinterest
pins or your imagination!

1920'S VS. 30'S

Hats in the 1930's were still worn close to the head but were often worn tilted and then evolved to have a more structured, boxy look.

SH°ES!

The 1920's was the first time in history that the shoe was so visible! Because hemlines exposed every part of a shoe, it was expected that shoes match an outfit, or a season (or both!).

Shoes of the 20's and 30's were covered in straps, buckles, embroidery, bling and other pretty decorations that set off a modest 2" heel. The basic structure of the shoe was the same for day and night so learning to draw it is easy. Once you know how to create the basic shoe shape, you can draw as many as you like, changing colors and decorations to your heart's content. Let's begin!

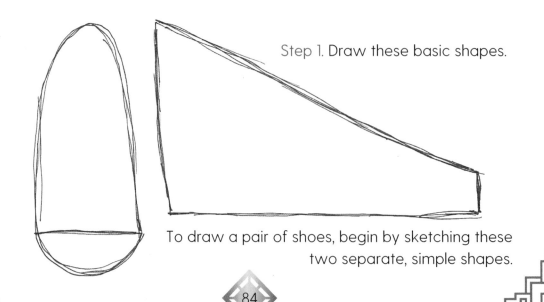

Step 1. Draw these basic shapes.

To draw a pair of shoes, begin by sketching these two separate, simple shapes.

BASIC CONSTRUCTION

Step 2. Define the shoe shape.

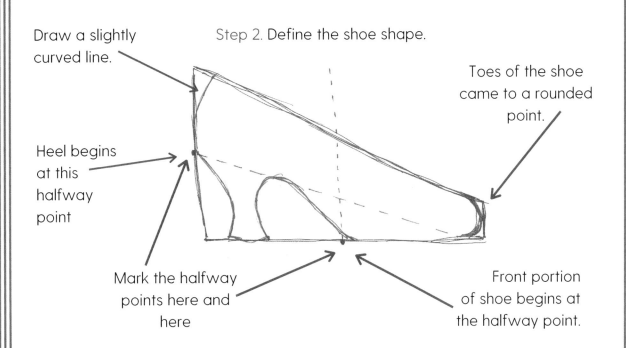

Draw a slightly curved line.

Heel begins at this halfway point

Mark the halfway points here and here

Toes of the shoe came to a rounded point.

Front portion of shoe begins at the halfway point.

Step 3. Determine shoe details.

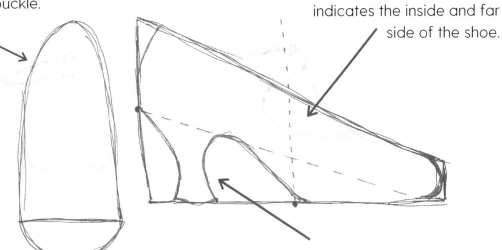

This is a typical Mary Jane style with single buckle.

Two lines drawn here indicates the inside and far side of the shoe.

Heals can be also be drawn as 2 straight lines (vs. the hourglass shape shown here).

Note: Step 3 is the part of your shoe drawing that will change the most as you try drawing different styles. Step 1 and 2 will remain the same.

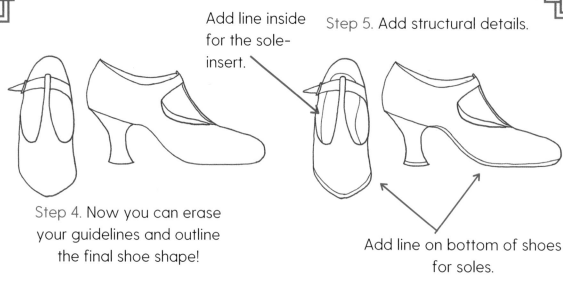

Add line inside for the sole-insert.

Step 5. Add structural details.

Step 4. Now you can erase your guidelines and outline the final shoe shape!

Add line on bottom of shoes for soles.

Step 6. Decorate to your hearts content!

Step 7. Add color!

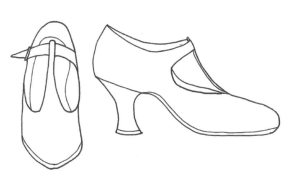

Easily return to **Step 3** in the drawing process to try creating some different styles!
This silhouette is the same for practically every style of shoe! If you can draw this shape then you can create both casual and fancy shoes with ease! Turn to the next page to get inspired!

Instead of a buckle and strap the top of the shoe is closed and laces are added.

Try a closed shoe like these Oxfords!

MORE STYLES TO DRAW!

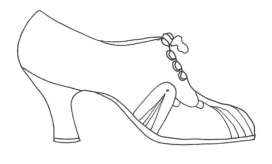

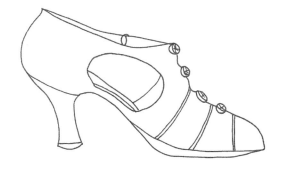

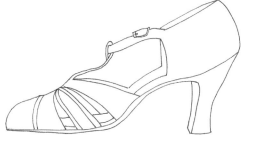

JEWELRY

Art Deco jewelry was very striking! Real, expensive stones were out and semi-precious and fake stones in geometric shapes were all the rage! Wearing jewelry had nothing to do with wealth and everything to do with decoration. During the day, it wasn't typical for ladies to wear any form of jewelry but when the sun went down and the dancing shoes went on, so too did those long strings of pearls, geometric dangle earrings, large rings and bangle bracelets! Let's draw some fun **earrings** first!

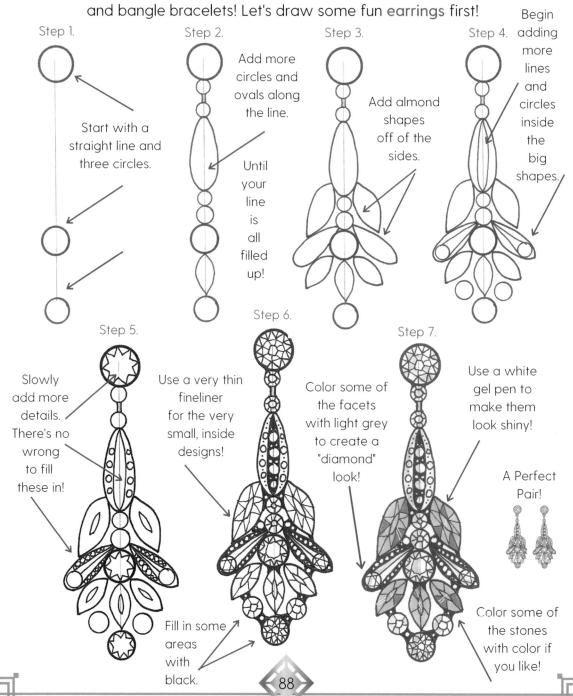

Step 1.

Start with a straight line and three circles.

Step 2.

Add more circles and ovals along the line.

Until your line is all filled up!

Step 3.

Add almond shapes off of the sides.

Step 4. Begin adding more lines and circles inside the big shapes.

Step 5.

Slowly add more details. There's no wrong to fill these in!

Step 6.

Use a very thin fineliner for the very small, inside designs!

Fill in some areas with black.

Step 7.

Color some of the facets with light grey to create a "diamond" look!

Use a white gel pen to make them look shiny!

A Perfect Pair!

Color some of the stones with color if you like!

Earrings are so fun to create aren't they? Let's make a few more fab pairs!

Step 1.

Step 2.

Step 3.

Step 4.

Step 5.

Start with top and bottom rectangles. Set height.

Add 3 circles at top. Thicken center line. Cut corners of lower shape.

Add lots of little circles and one small rectangle in bottom stone.

Add lots more little doodles! Add lines to create facets of the stones!

Color in the stone with a light base. Add darker shades, randomly. Add white highlight!

Step 1.

Step 2.

Step 3.

Step 4.

Step 5.

oooh la la!

RINGS!

Like earrings, rings of the Art Deco period are made up of gorgeous symmetry, geometric shapes, and loads of color! Follow the easy steps. Build on each geometric shape one line at a time! Let's draw!

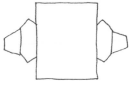

Step 1.

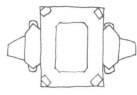

Step 2.

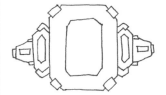

Step 3.

Step 4.

Step 5. The trick to making diamonds and silver look reflective is to leave lots of white! For the big stone, use various shades and white pen for highlights!

Step 1.

Step 2.

Step 3.

Step 4.

Step 5.

Step 6.

Step 7. Color! Use different shades of the same color to render the individual facets. The more random your color placement, the more realistic it appears!

Step 8. Use streaks of white pen to show pretty refracted highlights!

90

Step 1.

Step 2.

Step 3.

Step 4.

Step 5.

Step 6.

Creating these is quite like zentangling! Slowly add more intricate designs as you go!

Step 7.

I really want one of these rings!!

Step 1.

Step 2.

Step 3.

Step 4.

Step 5.

Who doesn't love a little bling?!

Step 6.

NECKLACES!

If Art Deco fashion conjures up the image of long strings of shiny pearls, wrapped lazily (and repeatedly) around slender necks and delicate wrists, you'd be spot on! Happily, drawing pearls is easy! Simply draw endless strands of circles! I'm more interested in learning to draw the fancier, more intricate necklaces. You know, the ones with fancy names like "Sautoirs" and "Lavalier" - words I had never heard before researching this era! And so, let's draw pearls...but also much, much more.

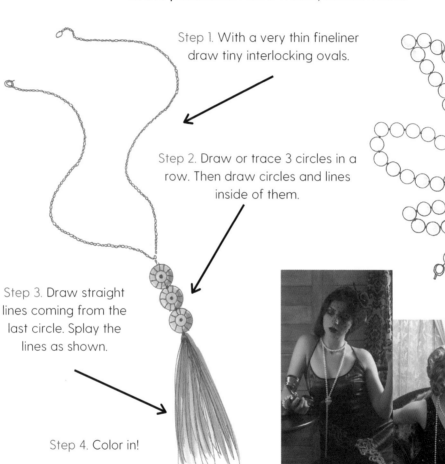

Step 1. With a very thin fineliner draw tiny interlocking ovals.

Step 2. Draw or trace 3 circles in a row. Then draw circles and lines inside of them.

Step 3. Draw straight lines coming from the last circle. Splay the lines as shown.

Step 4. Color in!

A Sautoir is simply a long necklace that ends in a tassle of some sort. You can find all different types of tassels from cheap beads to fabric strands to diamonds to a knot of pearls.

I just love this era. These long, drippy Lavalier necklaces with stunning pendants and dramatic endings weren't just worn down the front either. Often they were draped lazily (and deliberately) over a shoulder - or even sexier - dripped down a long, lean, bare back if a dress allowed (oh la la!). Makes me wonder why we ever stopped wearing necklaces that way?

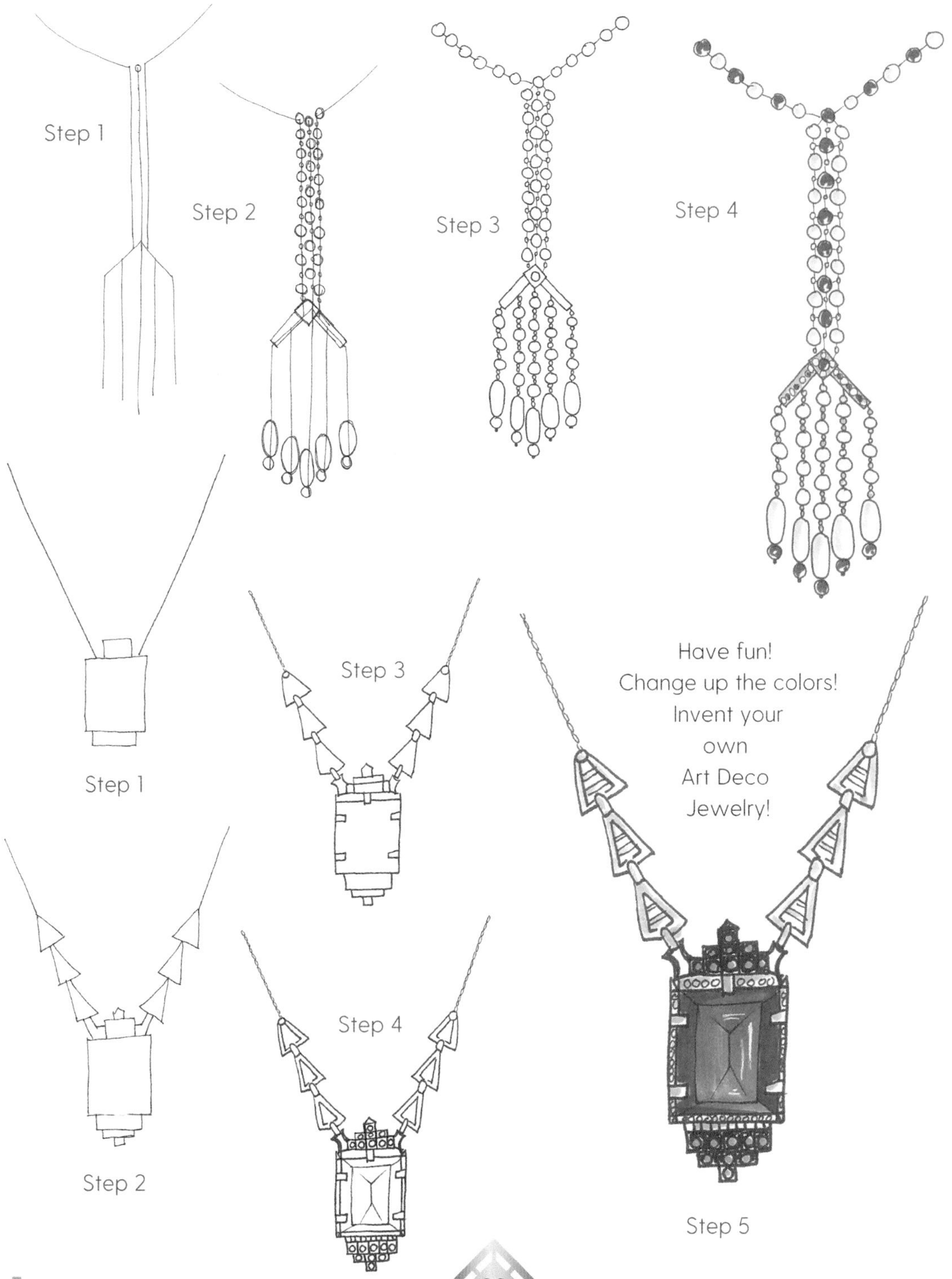

Step 1

Step 2

Step 3

Step 4

Step 1

Step 3

Step 2

Step 4

Have fun!
Change up the colors!
Invent your
own
Art Deco
Jewelry!

Step 5

93

BRACELETS & BANDEAUX

Bracelets were made out of every material imaginable from wood, plastic and coral, to diamonds, gold, jade and pearls! As far as women were concerned, the more bangles stacked, the better! Interestingly, the very popular "bandeau" (decorative headpiece) was oftentimes easily converted to bracelets or necklaces while not worn on the head.

We can use what we learned to draw necklaces and earrings to make bracelets and bandeaux! To create the look of the headpiece this flapper is wearing, first we can start with the small round clusters like this:

 Step 1. Draw circles. Use a template if you need to!

 Step 4. Draw 2 small squares around each center circle.

 Step 2. Draw smaller circles inside. Use a template if you need to!

 Step 5. Draw "V"s that connect the edges of the squares.

 Step 3. Draw smaller circles in the center of all them.

 Step 6. Use 3-4 shades of grey to create a shiny look!

Once you have your jewel flower created, you can string them together to make a bracelet or the bandeau shown! Or create a new configuration that's all yours!

This would make a gorgeous necklace too!

To make the center drop piece, double the floral and add a drop pearl or jewel!

Let's make another bracelet variation!

Step 1. Color the center jewel anything!

Step 2. Add side brackets.

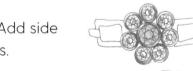

Step 3. Add links to make a ring.

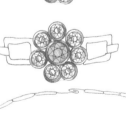

Step 4. Color in the stones and use greys to color the metal bits! So fun!

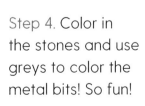

Or simply add looping circles with a very thin fineliner and now you have a whole new creation!

Here are some more popular bracelet styles. Cuffs got bigger and bangles stacked higher as the 20's made way into the 30's. How fun is that?!

Step 1. Freehand some ovals to make this easy bangle bracelet.

Step 2. Color beads with 2 shades of your favorite color.

Step 3. Add grey shadows and white highlights!

Step 1. Freehand some almond shapes with squares at the 2 ends.

Step 2. Draw diamonds inside and circles joining the almond pieces.

Step 3. Color metal parts with 2 shades of grey. Use the color of your choice for the stone!

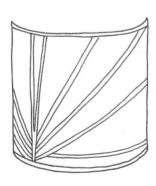 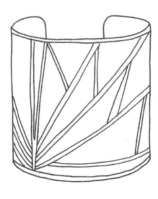 

Step 1. Draw a large rectangle that is curved up at the ends.

Step 2. Draw some fun, geometric patterns inside. Add lines at back.

Step 3. Color the metal in shades of grey and fill the larges spaces with bold colors!

3/4 PORTRAIT °F A FLAPPER!

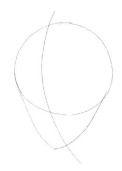

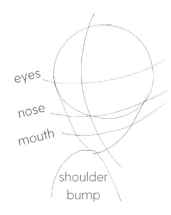

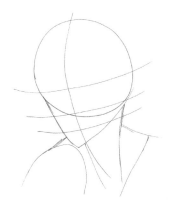

Step 1. Start with a circle. Add a "V" shape. Draw a curved line from top to bottom.

Step 2. Add 3 sweeping lines for the eyes, nose and mouth. Add a bump for the shoulder.

Step 3. Add 4 more lines to complete the neck and shoulders.

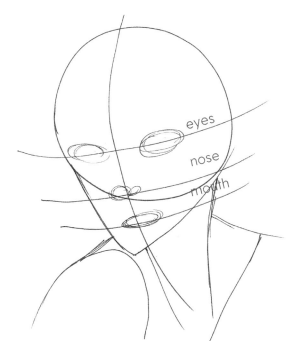

Step 4. Add ovals to approximate where the facial features will go.

Step 5. Define the features more (recommended adjustments shown here in red). Erase guidelines.

Step 6. Fineline the final face sketch. Draw a short, curly bob over top of head oval. Plan out the rough placement of headpiece.

Step 7. Fill out the major elements of the headpiece

Step 8. Add circles to fill in the headpiece ornamentation. Get ready for color! I am using Copic markers, you should use what you have and love!

Step 9. Use a light shade of hair, eye, skin and clothing color to color in the base layer.

Step 10. Add 2 shades of grey to the eyes. Use the darkest one around the entire eye area and on upper lid. Use lighter shade around a larger region, almost to the eyebrow.

Step 11. Add a darker shade of skin around eyes, on far side of nose, under chin and along hair line.

Step 12. Add lashes, eye sparkle (with white pen) and grey to the headpiece. Congratulations on a fabulous flapper!!!

I teach this (real-time) drawing in my Fun Fab Drawing Club!! Interested in joining? Visit AwesomeArtSchool.com for more information.

Turn the page and we'll do one more profile before we have to go!

LAST FABUL°US FLAPPER!

Step 1. Construct guidelines.

Use a plate or a bowl to help you trace a perfect circle!

Center line.

Profile (Diagonal) line.

Neck lines are at equal distance from centerline shown.

Step 2. Establish the Profile Line.

Note: The angle and distance of the Profile line can change dramatically depending on the person you are drawing, so if yours looks slightly different than mine, that's okay!

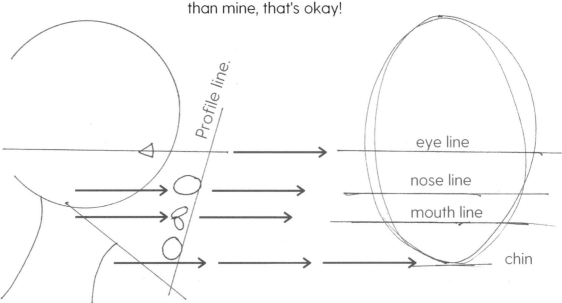

Profile line.

eye line

nose line

mouth line

chin

Step 3. Line up the guidelines in the same proportions that you would on a front facing portrait. Line up the "placeholder" ovals along the profile line.

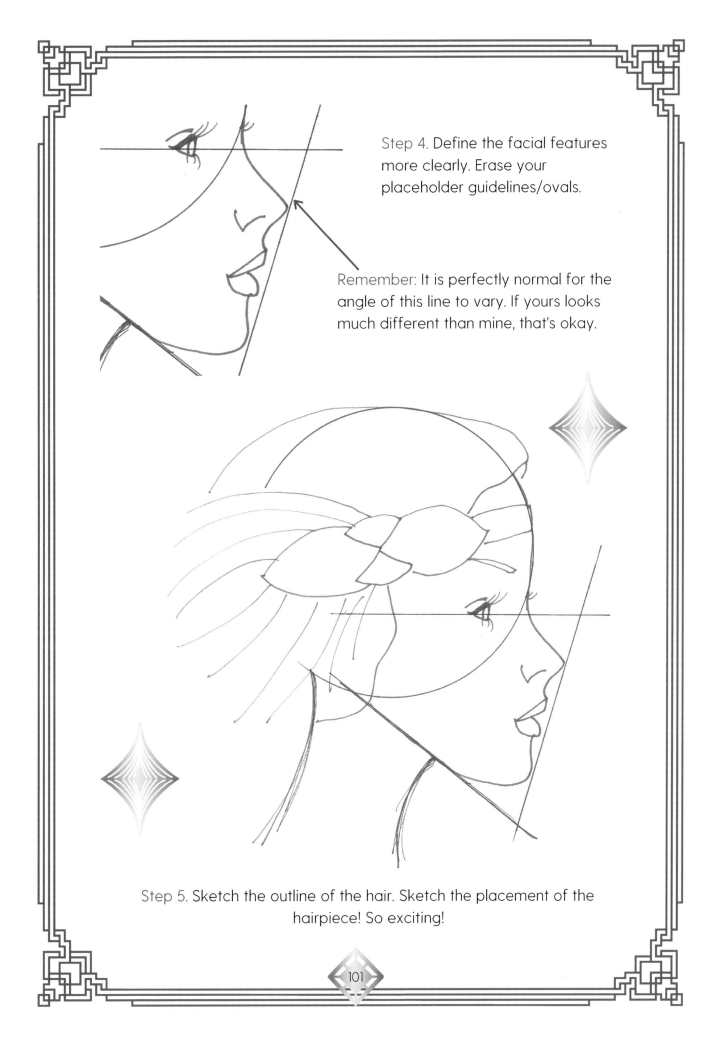

Step 4. Define the facial features more clearly. Erase your placeholder guidelines/ovals.

Remember: It is perfectly normal for the angle of this line to vary. If yours looks much different than mine, that's okay.

Step 5. Sketch the outline of the hair. Sketch the placement of the hairpiece! So exciting!

Step 6. Finalize the drawing by outlining with your fineliner.

Step 7. Add lots of feathers. Add an inside line to the side decorative pieces.

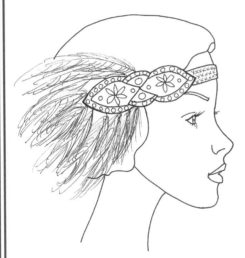

Step 8. Use a fineliner to add more decorations to the headpiece.

Step 9. Select 3 colors for the hair and skin. Layer each color, lightest to darkest, as you've been learning to do throughout the book!

Step 10. Add decorative strands off the headpiece with your fineliner, so pretty!

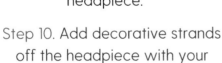

Drink a toast to YOU for a fabulous job well done!!

We draw lots **more** cocktails from the Prohibition in Vol 2! See you there!

ABOUT THE AUTHOR

Karen Campbell is a Boston area native who lives in North Carolina with her husband, three boy humans and three girl cats. She is a full time artist, instructor, business owner and is the author of many fun drawing and mixed media art books.

She started teaching art in 2011 and founded her online art school, Awesome Art School, in 2016. Thanks to her online art school and 2 art-based YouTube Channels, Karen has had the pleasure of impacting the lives of tens of thousands of adult learners across the globe with fun art lessons.

Her primary goal is to make art accessible to ANYONE with an interest and always keeps the primary focus on pure, unadulterated FUN!!! Subscribe to her Drawing YouTube channel for your own weekly dose: http://bit.ly/karendraws

MORE ART DECO FUN !

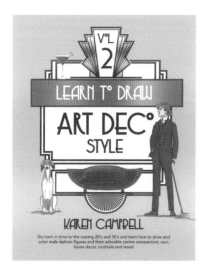

The vintage voyage continues with gentlemen, their canine companions, furniture, cars, cocktails and MORE!

Hundreds of large graphic Art Deco illustrations and designs for endless hours of coloring FUN! Come play!

MORE BOOKS BY KAREN CAMPBELL

 awesomeartschool.com

 karencampbellartist.com

 bit.ly/karendraws (drawing channel)

 youtube.com/karencampbellartist (mixed media)

 facebook.com/karencampbellartist

 instagram.com/karencampbellartist

 pinterest.com/karencampbellartist

 amazon.com/author/karencampbell

 etsy.com/shop/karencampbellartist

 patreon.com/karencampbellartist

Printed in Great Britain
by Amazon